In the name of God

***

Unwithering Flames: Book-1 "Shaheed Chamran; Narrated by His Wife" by: Habibeh Ja'farian
Copyright © 2023 Green Palm

All rights reserved. No portion of this book may be reproduced in any form without permission from the publisher. For permissions contact: info@Greenpalm.net
Translated and edited by: Green Palm books
Cover by Hossein Reza Vanaki
First Edition

To contribute towards future publications and be informed of the other books in the collection, please contact info@Greenpalm.net

Unwithering Flames

Book 1 - Chamran

In order to have a fruitful and prosperous relationship, people have come to terms that they must love one another. Unfortunately, the meaning of true love has been lost. Many have relegated love to just intimacy between a man and a woman. However, this is just the initial stage of true love, and we must aspire to reach a higher level beyond mere physical attraction. Such love is built on the foundation of honesty, enjoyment, selflessness, and spiritual attainment. Although many strive to reach this transcendent form of love, the affairs of this world become a barrier for them.

This series of books entitled Unwithering Flames recounts to us stories of those men and women who in the events of the Islamic Revolution and the Iraq's war against Iran turned away from this world just for the sake of God. In doing so, they became lovers in the true sense. They had the type of love that did not just make the pain of this world bearable, rather it was something beautiful for them. The love whose flame has not dimmed even with martyrdom or death.

 www.GREENPALM.net

 +98 999 99 16 140

 info@GREENPALM.net

SYNOPSIS

The story of Ghada Jaber is the story of a wealthy Lebanese merchant's daughter who although despised war, fell in love with a scholarly freedom fighter from Iran who actively participated in the war, and would also teach in the orphanages of the Lebanese Shias. Her troubles had only just begun; she had to communicate with everyone, from her mother and father to her family that she wanted to leave behind her life of luxury and safety, and instead wanted to take a path that would lead her to a life of hardship and poverty. This was all for the sake of the Shaheed Mustafa Chamran.

Not everyone knows of Chamran, however, Ghada is a different story. She not only knew him but knew him intimately. The Chamran who she spent five years of her life with, despite everything that happened remained the same. Throughout all of the events: living under constant Israeli bombardment in the south of Lebanon, the schools of Amal, his participation in the Islamic Revolution of Iran, the time he spent as the defense minister, and his battles against the ruthless Komalas of Kurdistan, Chamran's love and devotion for her never decreased a little bit. Now, even though Chamran's body is no longer by her side, his spirit will be forever intertwined with hers.

Contents

Chapter 1
The Candle..9

Chapter 2
The Mere Act of God!..................................27

Chapter 3
A Stranger in Iran!......................................47

Chapter 4
I Will Be Martyred Tomorrow................65

Chapter 1
The Candle

The girl rolled the pen between her fingers and finally wrote the following sentence on a piece of paper she had been staring at all night long: "I hate war." She burst into laughter, though. Her heart was full of sorrow; is there anyone who might like war? She had no idea. Of course not. She was a journalist, a poet, and had even written a book. She hadn't traveled much but she knew Lagos in Africa because that's where she was born. She also knew some European cities because she had traveled there before. Her dad traded pearls between Africa and Japan, and the family spent money like water. Nevertheless, she was Lebanese enough to know that Lebanon was a fertile land for war as it was for olive and palm, though she didn't know why.

I couldn't understand why people should kill each other. I didn't even know what could be done to change the present condition. I was just sad about civil war and disaster. We had a beautiful house in Tyre with two floors, a yard, and a balcony facing the sea, which Israel destroyed later. I would sit on this balcony at night, cry, and write. I talked to the sea, the fish, and the sky about this so-called Islamic war. These conversations were published as poems and articles in newspapers. Mustafa had seen my name below these writings. I had heard his name, too. But that was it. I didn't know anything about him. I had never seen him. However, I thought him to be a tough fighter who contributed to this war.

It all began when Sayyed Mohammad Gharavi, the clergyman of our city, came to me and said that Imam Musa al-Sadr[1]

---

1. Sayyid Musa al-Sadr (b. 1928), known as Imam Musa al-Sadr, was a Shia leader in Lebanon and a founder of the Supreme Islamic Shia Council in Lebanon and Amal Movement. In 1978, he visited

would like to see me. I wasn't spiritually ready to see anyone at that time, especially when it came to that name. But Sayyed Gharavi insisted that I go see Imam Musa Sadr, who was described as a man who loved reading. Finally, after Sayyed Gharavi's insistence, I reluctantly accepted. One day, I went to the Supreme Council for Islamic Revolution (Shia[2] party in Lebanon) to see Imam Musa Sadr. He welcomed me warmly and complimented me on my writings and how well I wrote about *wilayah*[3] and Imam

---

Libya upon an official invitation by its president at the time, Muammar al-Gaddafi, but never returned. According to some evidence and reports, he was imprisoned or martyred by al-Gaddafi.

2. Shiism is a major Islamic denomination along with Sunnism. Shias believe that imamate is just like prophethood appointed by God, and the Imam is in charge of people's guidance after the Prophet's demise. According to Shias, at the command of God, the Prophet (s) appointed 'Ali b. Abi Talib (a) and eleven people from his progeny as the Imams and leaders of the Islamic community after him. The word 'Shia' literally means the 'follower'.

3. Guardianship (wilayah) is God's right to be the master and guardian of His servants. According to Shias, the right is transferred to the Prophet (s) and the Infallible Imams (a) as well.

Hussain, who I love immensely. "What are you up to now? Universities are closed", he asked. "I teach at a girls' high school", I replied. "Leave your job and come work with us", he said. "What kind of work?" I asked. "You are a great writer. You can write beautifully about Imam Hussain, Lebanon, and many other things. Well, why don't you come and write about them?" he said. "I can't leave the high school; I mean, I don't want to", I replied. "We will give you more money; just come work with us", he said. That remark upset me. "I don't work for money, I'm passionate about people". I said. I then angrily left the place. He was an honorable man, and so he followed me and apologized. Then, unexpectedly, he asked me if I knew Chamran. I said I had heard his name. He said I should see him. "I am mad about this war, about all this bloodshed and turmoil. I can't meet those involved in this war", I said. Imam Musa assured me that Chamran was not like that. "He was looking for you. We have an orphanage. I think this job would be suitable for you. I would like you to go there and meet Chamran", he said. He didn't allow me to leave until I promised that I would go there.

Six or seven months had passed since I made that promise, and I hadn't gone. Wherever Sayyed Gharavi saw me, he asked me why I hadn't been and that Imam Musa Sadr had asked about me. But I wasn't ready at the time. Chamran's name reminded me of war and so I didn't think I would be able to meet him.

Simultaneously, my father had a heart problem and I was distraught. One night Sayyed Gharavi came to our home to visit my father. While he was leaving, he gave me a calendar of the Amal movement[4]. He said that it was a gift. I didn't pay much attention to it, but I glanced at it at night while I was writing. It had twelve paintings for the twelve months; all beautiful. But there wasn't any name or signature below them. One of the paintings had a completely dark background, and in the middle, there was a candle burning with a weak flame, which wasn't strong enough to lighten the

---

4. The Amal Movement is a political Shia organization in Lebanon, which was established in 1974 by Imam Musa al-Sadr, in defense of Lebanese Shias through military fights against the Zionist regime. Imam Musa al-Sadr and shaheed Mustafa Chamran were the early leaders of the movement.

darkness. Below the painting, there was a poetic sentence in Arabic saying: "I may not be able to eradicate this darkness, but with this little light, I will show the difference between darkness and light, truth and falsehood. And the one who seeks the light, however small that light might be, it will grow in their heart." I cried a lot that night. It was as if that light had engulfed me. But I didn't know who painted it.

One day, I went to the institute with one of my friends who also wanted to visit. On the first floor, they introduced me to a man and said he was Dr. Chamran. Mustafa was wearing a smile which surprised me. I thought someone whose name was associated with war and everybody was scared of must be heartless. I was scared, too, but his smile and calm demeanor surprised me. My friend introduced me to him. "So, you are Ghada Jaber. I was waiting for your visit, I expected to see you sooner." He spoke to me as if he knew me from before, it was strange. "Are you sure this is Dr. Chamran?" I asked my friend. She was sure. Mustafa brought a calendar just like the one Sayyed Gharavi had given me a few weeks before. I looked at it. "I have seen it before", I said. "Have you seen all the paintings? Which one did you like the most?" Mustafa asked. "The candle, I was moved by it". I replied.

My answer caught his attention. "The candle? Why the candle?" he asked. I cried involuntarily, and my tears poured down my face. "I'm not sure. This candle, this light; it is as if I can feel it in my soul. I didn't think anyone could perceive and relay the meaning of a candle and sacrifice as beautifully as this", I said. "I didn't think a Lebanese girl would be able to perceive a candle and its meaning as perfectly as this, either", Mustafa said. "Who painted this? I would like to meet and get to know that person", I asked. "Me", Mustafa replied. I was shocked now more than the moment I saw his smile and face. "You?! You painted it?" I asked. "Yes, I painted it", Mustafa replied. "But you live in war and are surrounded by blood, how is it possible that you have such strong feelings?" I asked. Then, something more unusual happened. Mustafa started to read my writings aloud. "I have read all of your works and have flown with your soul from afar", Mustafa said. Then he began shedding tears. This was the first time we met, and it was stunning.

The second time I saw him I was completely ready to work in the institute.

Gradually, we got to know each other more. Mustafa and I were together quite often; in the institute with the children, in various cities, and once or twice at the war front. To me his deeds were all impressive and informative, without him intending them to be so.

> *Ghada had been raised under the influence of European culture. She was not wearing a proper hijab, but she wanted to be different to see something other than this extravagance. She likes this house that has only one room whose door always welcomes everyone. Children can come in at any hour, sit on the floor, and chat with their principal. Mustafa received her in the same room, and Ghada was astonished when she found out that she must take off her shoes and sit on the floor. In her opinion Mustafa was a masterpiece, surprising and charming.*

I remember that I was with him on one of his trips to the villages and he gave me a gift in the car. It was his first gift to me before we got married. It made me happy and I opened it immediately. The gift was a scarf, a red one with large flowers. I was moved, but he smiled and said that the children liked to see me wearing a scarf. Since then, I have always worn a scarf. I knew the children would criticize Mustafa for bringing a woman into the institute. But it seemed strange that Mustafa tried hard to draw me closer to the children. "She is a good woman. She comes to the institute because of you. She wants to learn from you. God willing, we will teach her ourselves", he said. He hadn't said I wasn't wearing proper hijab, that I wasn't like them, or that there was something wrong with my family and relatives. It was his attitude that influenced me. As if I was an infant, he pushed me forward step by step and made me familiar with Islam. We were together for nine beautiful months before we got married. Our marriage was met with many severe issues.

"You are crazy! This man is twenty years older than you. He is Iranian. He has always been in the war zone. He doesn't have any money. He is not like us. He doesn't even have a birth certificate!"

Ghada placed her head between her hands and closed her eyes. Why had everyone become so similar? It was as if those words were the text of a play everyone had memorized, including her; her mother, father, relatives, and even her friends, except for her. She wished she had been born into an ordinary family. She wished she had no car of her own! She wished her father was a teacher or a worker instead of trading between Africa and Japan. Everything would have been different. She knew that Mustafa's situation was not any better than hers. Those who work with Mustafa didn't like him. They reject him…O God! This is the most challenging part of the story. She wished her grandmother was there. If she were there, Ghada would have nothing to worry about. Her grandma would listen and sympathize with her. She remembered the tale of her grandmother's life during her years with her husband and two daughters in Palestine. A young Sunni man falls in love with one of the daughters and is met with no objection. But the young man chooses the Day of Ashura[5] for a marriage proposal and prenuptial agreements. Grandma gets upset

---

5. The Day of Ashura is the tenth of Muharram (the first lunar month in the Hijri calendar). On the Day of Ashura in 61 AH/October 13, 680, Imam al-Hussain (a), the third Shia Imam, was martyred along with his companions in Karbala by the army of Yazid, the Umayyad caliph, in an unequal war while he was thirsty.

and rejects the young suitor. But the grandpa, who did not care for such issues, wanted to hold the wedding ceremony.

Grandma did not hesitate and one day she sat on a horse and came to this side of the border, to Tyre.

> Grandma wore a burqa, held mourning gatherings for Imam Hussain (a) at her home, and had memorized many prayers. She raised Ghada and taught her prayers. If she could see that Ziyarat Ashura[6], al-Sahifa al-Sajjadiyya[7], and all those prayers Ghada loves and says before she goes to bed are now deeply ingrained in Mustafa, she wouldn't hesitate in giving her blessing for their marriage.

---

6. Ziyarat Ashura is a salutatory supplication addressed to Imam al-Hussain (a), the third Shia Imam. This is widely recited by Shia, and is recommended to be recited frequently.

7. Al-Sahifa al-Sajjadiyya is a book including the available supplications of Imam al-Sajjad (a), the fourth Shia Imam. After the Qur'an and Nahj al-Balagha, it is the most venerated Shia text., which is also known as "Zabur Al Muhammad" (the Psalms of Muhammad's household) and "Injil Ahl al-Bayt" (the Gospel of the Prophet's household).

Above all, Mustafa's love for *Wilayah* was what attracted me to him. I always wrote that the Tyre Sea and every particle of Jabal Amel's soil reminded me of Abu Dharr's[8] voice. This voice was in my soul and I felt like I had to reach there, but there was no one to take my hand. Mustafa played the role of that "hand." When he came into my life, it was as if Salman[9] came. "Salman is from us, the Ahl al-Bayt (our household)". He could take my hand and drag me out of this darkness out of this monotonous life. I couldn't convince myself to get married and live like millions of others. I was looking for a man like Mustafa, a great soul, free from the world and all its belongings. But my parents and relatives couldn't understand this. They had different ideals and had the right to say 'No'. They looked at Mustafa's financial circumstance; he had nothing of

---

8. Abu Dharr al-Ghifari (d. 32 AH/653) was one of the first companions of the Prophet (s), a Shia and an advocate of the caliphate of Imam ʿAli (a).

9. Salman al-Farsi (d. 33 AH) was a well-known Persian companion of the Prophet (s). The Prophet (s) referred to him as a member of his own household, saying, "Salman is from us, the people of the house" and "the heaven is passionate for Salman."

material value. A man who doesn't have any money, any home, any life…nothing! This is what they paid attention to. Unfortunately, the Lebanese society has remained like this up until today. Appearance and money define how valuable a person is. They respect those who are fashionable in their dress, and if he is a doctor, he must own a high-end car. Spirituality and such things never attract anyone's attention. However, Mustafa asked for my hand by sending Sayyed Gharavi to my family. My family rejected it at first, but Imam Musa Sadr intervened. "I vouch for him. If my daughter had reached the age of marriage, I wouldn't have hesitated to accept his proposal," he said. His words impressed them, but the conflict was still unresolved. They didn't give in, and I didn't, either. I had already made up my mind to marry Mustafa. I thought it was a good idea to finally sign our marriage contract with Imam Musa Sadr's permission as a religious leader, but Mustafa disagreed. Despite all the pressures, he insisted that my parents sign our marriage contract. "Try to convince them kindly. I wouldn't like to marry you while your parents are upset," said Mustafa. Despite his feelings and unique personality, he was always submissive to my parents and he was cautious not to hurt them over this issue. The first, and perhaps the last time he shouted at me, was because of them.

There were days when the south of Lebanon was repeatedly bombed and everyone had evacuated. I was in Beirut, but Mustafa had stayed in the south with his colleagues. I had grown interested in all of them and so I couldn't wait to see them. I went to the Supreme Islamic Shi'ite Council to Imam Musa, and asked him about Mustafa and his colleagues. Imam Musa Sadr gave me a letter and told me to deliver it to Dr. Chamran as soon as possible. Under the heavy fire of artillery and mortars, Professor Yousef Hosseini and I went to the institute. When we arrived, they told us that Dr. Chamran wasn't there and that they didn't know where he was. We spent so much time looking for him and we finally found him in "El Kharayeb." He was surprised, he didn't expect me. They were facing a difficult situation, all those bombs, mortar shells, etc. It was perilous. Mustafa took the letter, wrote a reply, and gave it to me to deliver to Imam Musa Sadr. "I don't want to go, I'll stay here. I won't return to Beirut," I said. Mustafa insistently asked me to return to Beirut as soon as possible, but I didn't want to return. That was the moment when Mustafa, with all his gentleness and kindness, got angry for the first time. "Get into the car! It's a war, it's not a joke!" he shouted at me. I was scared and upset. It wasn't good, but he gave me a military command. However, I didn't expect him to yell at me in front of the men and tell me to leave immediately!

When I decided to leave, Mustafa came to us. "You go, I'll take her in my car," said Mustafa to Yousef Hosseini. I cried from El Kharayeb to Sidon. "I thought you were a very gentle person. I couldn't imagine you would treat me like that," I told Mustafa. He didn't say a word until we arrived at Sidon, where I was supposed to be transferred to Yousef Hosseini's car to return to Beirut. There, Mustafa apologized to me, just like the person I knew. "I didn't mean it; I don't want you to come and stay here without your family's permission. You should go back and stay with them," he said.

From then on, we had a hard time. I wasn't allowed to go out. After eighteen years of going out alone, they took away my car keys. My brother took me wherever I wanted to go and brought me back, just so that I don't go to the school or to Mr.

Gharavi. Poor Sayyed Gharavi! He went through a lot because of my marriage. My parents told him "You are the one who introduced our daughter to that man". I always managed to meet Mustafa despite all difficulties. But lately, he had become very frustrated and angry. "Everyone is talking about us. There is too much pressure on us. You must make a decision. Either this way or that way, stop it please," he said one day. Mustafa's words made me more upset. I had to choose between my parents – whom I loved so much – and him. It was a real dilemma, much more difficult than I thought. "Mustafa! If you leave me, I'll choose them. You need to help me!" I said. "Well. This situation cannot go on this way," he said.

When I got home that night, my parents were watching TV. I turned off the TV. "Father! I have never upset or annoyed you during all these twenty-five or twenty-six years. But for the first time in my life, I want to be disobedient, and I do apologize for this." I said without thinking. I hadn't spoken about my relationship with Mustafa for a while, so my father thought it was all over. "What's the matter? Why?" he asked. "We are going to get married the day after tomorrow," I said abruptly without having already talked about it with Mustafa. They were stunned. "I made my mind to marry Mustafa. We will sign our marriage contract in the presence of Imam Musa Sadr." I continued. I was wondering where all that courage came from! Mustafa had no idea what I was doing.

My mother became furious. She stood up and started yelling at me. It was the first time she wanted to beat me. My father intervened and asked me quietly who I was going to marry. "Dr. Chamran. I tried so hard to convince you, but I failed. Mustafa told me that it was not going to work anymore and wanted to leave for a trip," I said. My father listened to me. "I have always provided you with everything you needed. But I see that this man is not right for you. He is not like us. We don't know his family. It would help if you didn't get married to him for your own sake," he said quietly. "But I have already made up my mind and I will go. Imam Musa Sadr has also allowed me to do it. He is a religious leader and can grant the permission," I said. My father realized that it was severe. "Why the day after tomorrow? We are a prestigious family," he said. "We have made our decision, and it must be the day after tomorrow. I have also told Imam Musa Sadr that I want the marriage contract to be signed in my father's house, not somewhere else. I would be much happier if you agree and support us," I said. "But you need to be ready for something like this," said my father. "I am ready, completely!" I said.

I had no idea where all that decisiveness and courage came from. I was leaving everything behind. Though, I didn't realize it then, I was not even pious enough to do that. I just saw that Mustafa was a great and gentle man who loved Ahl al-Bayt [The Holy Household], and I loved all these things, too.

"OK. If that's what you want, I won't disagree," said my father. I couldn't believe that father so readily agreed. How should I inform Mustafa then?

Chapter 2
The Mere Act of God!

What if she has to take her words back! What if her father changes his mind in the coming days! Where is Mustafa? She looked for Mustafa all around the city and village until she finally found him. "We will sign the marriage contract tomorrow. My father gave in," she said. Mustafa couldn't believe it, it was extraordinary! Now, when she thinks about those days, she wonders if she was the one who did all those things. No, it was not her, it was God, the mere act of God. It was Mustafa's charisma shining on her unknowingly. Knowledge came later on… She suddenly laughed, as if something was tickling her fancy. She didn't even notice that Mustafa was bald! Two months after their marriage, her friend raised the question: "Ghada! There is something in your marriage that is unknown to me. You were too fussy about your suitors. "He is tall; he is short ..." It seemed you wanted a man with perfect looks and appearance. Now I wonder how you've chosen Dr. Chamran, a bald man!" Ghada remembered the shocked look on her own face as her friend spoke. She took offense and argued that Mustafa wasn't bald. Her friend thought she was crazy, unable to notice Mustafa's baldness.

The very day she got home, she opened the door and saw Mustafa. She then started to laugh. "Why are you laughing?" asked Mustafa. "Mustafa, you're bald? I didn't know!" she said as she cried tears of laughter. Mustafa started to laugh, too. He even told the story to Imam Musa Sadr. Since then, Mr. Sadr always asked Mustafa about what he did which caused Ghada not to notice his appearance.

This story may be funny, but it really happened. The moments I was with

Mustafa, both before and after marriage, I was far removed from worldly concerns. "I don't want a wedding ceremony, just invite the close relatives, uncles, etc.," I told my father. "It's none of my concern. Do as you please," said my father. The morning of the day we wanted to sign our marriage contract, I got ready to teach at the high school. My mother didn't speak to me. She was angry. "Where are you going?" asked my sister. "To the high school," I replied. "You have to go to the hairdresser's and put on make-up now," she said. Did I go to the hairdresser? Never! I went to high school. Everyone there asked me why I came. "Why not? Mustafa wants me just the way I am," I said. When I returned home from the high school, the guests had already arrived. Mustafa had no relatives there so Sayyed Gharavi and Imam Musa Sadr's son-in-law, his family, and his sisters had come on his behalf. Many of my relatives were absent because they were all upset and against our marriage.

"What are you going to wear?" my sister asked. "I have a lot of clothes," I replied. "It must be suitable for the ceremony," she said. That afternoon, she bought me a suitable dress. Everyone said that I was crazy and that they didn't want to lose their prestige amongst their relatives. I was probably the first bride who didn't care about wearing make-up. The ceremony was held in the presence of those few guests. The groom was then called to come forward and offer a gift to the bride. This is our custom every groom must give a ring to the bride.

I hadn't even thought about this moment. Mustafa entered and brought a gift. I went forward and opened it. It was a candle. He gave me only a candle as a wedding gift. There was a beautiful text written next to it. I quickly hid the gift. Everyone began to ask what it was. "I can't show it to you," I said. If they knew it was a candle, they would think the groom was crazy. Giving a candle as an engagement gift to the bride was considered strange. "Where is the groom? He should come forward and offer the bride a ring," said my sister. "It is not a ring," I said softly. My sister got angry. "You want to send mom to the hospital tonight? Who has seen an engagement ceremony without a ring? What kind of engagement is this? We lost our prestige amongst the others," she said. "Well, there is no ring. What shall I do now? I don't care!" I exclaimed. Finally, we looked into our mother's closet. I wore her ring and came out of the room.

My mahr[10] was the Holy Quran and a commitment made by the groom to guide me through the path of transcendence, Ahl al-Bayt (a), and Islam. It was the first wedding in Tyre with such a mahr; there was no money involved. To my relatives and the people around us, it seemed weird.

My mother realized that the ring I was wearing was hers and she was distraught. "Mom, I wasn't in my senses; otherwise, I would have told Mustafa to buy a ring, and he would certainly have bought it," I said. "Where is he going to take you now? Where are you going to live?" asked my mother. "I want to go to the institute where the others also live," I said. My mother had visited the place. It was just a room with a few fruit boxes instead of a bed. "Is this where my daughter will end up? Were you disabled? Didn't you have hands and eyes that you put yourself in this situation?" asked my mother. But I didn't care about any of those things. I wanted to live there as it was, on the ground. "I will buy you home appliances, and I won't let anyone, even the relatives and

---

10. Mahr, the bridal gift determined before marriage in Islam.

others, know about it," said my mother. In Lebanon, it is not customary for a bride to take anything to the groom's house, including her dowry. People would spread a rumor that the bride's family paid money to be rid of their daughter. Mustafa and I didn't accept it. We wanted to live without those things.

"Why are you still here? Take your stuff and let's go to our own house," said Mustafa one afternoon when he came to see me. "Sure!" I said. I put my toothbrush, comb, etc., in a plastic bag and told my mother I am leaving. "Where are you going?" asked my mother. "To my husband's house," I replied. This is the simplicity with which I wanted to go to my husband's house. I didn't consider family honor or things like that with great regard. My mother thought I was kidding. "I will come back tomorrow to take the remaining belongings," I continued. My mother got angry. She shouted at Mustafa and spoke harshly to him. "You have made my daughter insane! You have mesmerized her! You…" shouted my mother. Then she went into a state of shock and fell to the floor. Mustafa hugged and kissed her. My mother's hands and feet were trembling, she was shocked as to what was happening to her. "You made my daughter insane! Divorce her right now. Break your spell and set her free," said my mother angrily. She did not mean what she was saying. We were shocked, too. Mustafa tried to calm her down, but it only worsened the situation, and she didn't stop. "OK. I'll divorce her," Mustafa said. "Right now!" insisted my mother. "I'll divorce her right now," Mustafa finally said. "Will you promise me?" asked my mother, as if she didn't believe him. "I'll promise to divorce her right now, but only on one condition!" replied Mustafa. I was petrified, we were about to be divorced. My mother wasn't feeling well. "I'll divorce her, provided she agrees. I don't want you to be so upset." said Mustafa. My mom turned to me and asked me to say I want to get divorced. "OK, mom! I'll get divorced tomorrow," I said. That night, I didn't go with Mustafa. My mother calmed down, and two days later, when my father came back from his trip, they told him the whole story. My father was a very rational man. Before he arrived, my mother was not going to change her mind, and she was still insistently asking me to get divorced. "We have no such a thing as getting divorced in our family. However, if you are determined to do that, now is the time. But if you want to continue with this under these circumstances...," my father told me. "Yes, I accept all of the conditions," I said. "Then go. We don't want to see you anymore. Please, just no longer trouble us," he continued.

To Ghada, those words were unbelievably harsh... She turned back and looked at Mustafa's side profile walking beside her. She thought that Mustafa was worth it. Despite all these problems, dear Mustafa always lets her see her mother whenever she wants.

Mustafa's voice brought her back to reality. "I won't come back to your home today. Try to win your mother's heart. If she said something unpleasant, don't get upset. I'll come to pick you up at night," said Mustafa.

Mom felt very sick that night. She had a kidney failure. "Mom is not feeling well. I'm worried about her, I can't leave her," I told Mustafa when he came to pick me up. Mustafa came to her. He saw she was in so much pain and tears streamed down his face. He kissed my mom's hand and said, "tell me what you're feeling."

A doctor visited her and said that she had to be hospitalized in Beirut. At the time, Israel was repeatedly bombarding Beirut and Tyre, and it was so difficult to travel back and forth between the two cities. "I'll take her," Mustafa said. Then he lifted mother into his arms, and we went to Beirut. Mother was hospitalized for a week. Mustafa recommended that I should look after my mother and never leave her alone, even at night. "You are alone. Why do you make Ghada stay here? Take her! I'll take care of myself," mother said whenever she woke up and saw Mustafa there. "No, she should stay here and look after you. I'll stay, too, for as long as I can," Mustafa said. He then kissed my mother's hands and cried. He cried a lot. Mother was surprised and ashamed to receive that much kindness.

My mother's health improved, and we went back home. I stayed with her for two more days. I remember the day Mustafa came to pick me up. Before starting the car, he grabbed my hand and kissed it. He kept kissing it and thanking me with tearful eyes. "Why are you doing this, Mustafa?" I asked. "The hands that serve mothers are sacred to me, and they should be kissed," he replied. "Why are you thanking me? The person I served was my mother, not yours. Why are you doing this?" I asked. "Hands that serve mothers are sacred, and those who are not kind to their mothers are not kind to anyone. I thank you for serving your mother with such love and affection," he said. "Mustafa! You are saying this after all they did to you?" I said. "They had every right to, because they love you. They don't know me, and naturally, every parent wants to keep their daughter safe," he said. I never forgot how valuable serving my mother was for him. My mother changed drastically after all this.

"I was wrong saying that. I take my words back. She must do this for you. Why do you keep spoiling her so much?"

Mustafa didn't say anything. He just laughed. Ghada looked at her mom. "Now, she is more sympathetic to Mustafa than me," She thought to herself. Her heart relished such a thought. The day Mustafa came to their house for a marriage proposal, my mother asked him if he knew the girl he wanted to marry. "Every morning she wakes up before she even washes her face and brushes her teeth, someone makes her bed, brings a glass of milk to her bedroom, and makes coffee. You can't live with such a girl. You can't bring her a maid in this situation," mother said to

Mustafa. "I can't bring her a maid, but I'll promise to make her bed and serve her with a glass of milk and a cup of coffee on a tray in her bed, as long as I'm alive," he said after listening quietly to my mother.

And so he did until the day of his martyrdom. Even in Ahvaz[11], on the war front, he insisted on making my bed. He fetched milk. He didn't drink coffee, but he made it because he knew that we, the Lebanese people, are accustomed to drinking coffee. "Well, why, Mustafa?" I asked. "I have promised your mother to do this for you as long as I'm alive," he said. Mother always thought that after marriage, Mustafa would retaliate and stop me from visiting them. However, Mustafa did nothing except show kindness and respect. I sometimes thought he was so tolerant that he could make room for the whole universe in his soul and at the same time bear all the difficulties we faced at the Jabal Amel School.

---

11. Ahvaz is a major historical city in Iran and the capital of Khuzestan Province in southwestern Iran. It was the main headquarters of the Iranian army in the Iraqi war on Iran. It was a target of frequent missile and air strikes of the Iraqi army.

Our home consisted of two rooms inside the school itself, along with 400 orphans. It was also a base for the Amal organization. It did not seem like an everyday life anymore, there was no peace. But Mustafa and I knew from the very beginning that our marriage was not an ordinary one. I felt his character was the only thing that mattered. I considered myself the closest person to him, and all those with him thought so, too. Sometimes it seemed as if the whole world and all the moral virtues that a perfect man, a humble exemplification of Imam Ali (a) could have, had been accumulated in the corner of that school, in these two rooms. However, he was very lonely. As his wife, a new aspect of his soul would gradually open up for me. That's how he was, he revealed his character step by step. Had he told his expectations or things he gradually made me progress in from the first day, I would have failed. He brought me along with love and slowly but surely opened up different aspects to me.

I talked to him about the things I was ashamed of even thinking about or expressing. He was closer to me than I was to myself. The school children were the same way. They felt oneness with him.

The organization was a base for the people of the south. It was such that whenever someone entered, they would feel a sense of peace. Mustafa didn't want the school to be an orphanage. He paid regular visits to the four floors of the dormitory and cried after he came back. "Instead of getting help and being raised by their mothers, they have been scattered. The dormitory is like a prison. I can't tolerate seeing them living here," he said.

I remember the first Eid after our marriage. In Lebanon, it's customary for people to gather together, but Mustafa stayed at the institute and didn't come to my father's house. "I would like to know why you didn't go," I asked him that night. "It's Eid today. Most of the children are with their families now. When those who have left return, they will talk about their time with the 200-300 children who have remained at the school. I should stay to have lunch with them and amuse them so that they can have something to talk about as well," he said. "Why did not you eat the food my mom sent? Why did you merely eat bread and cheese with tea?" I asked. "This is not the food served at the school," he said. "You were late. The children would not notice what you ate." I said. "But God would see it," he said with tearful eyes.

> *As soon as he entered the school, he was surrounded by a swarm of children like the bees of a hive. Mustafa was their father, friend, and playmate. "Look how strong these children are! They are lion cubs," Mustafa said. Ghada could see how passionately he spoke and how shiny his eyes became. He was happy when they were happy and restless when they were sad. From time to time, when they got in Ghada's worn out Volvo and drove from one village to another, Mustafa would always get off the car in the middle of the road upon seeing a child sitting and crying by the roadside. He got out of the car, hugged the child, wiped his face with a handkerchief, and kissed him. Soon after that, his tears would flow. The first time, Ghada thought he knew the child. "No, I don't. The only thing that matters is that this child is Shia. He's been suffering from 1300 years of oppression. His crying dates back to all the oppression the Shia of Imam Ali (a) have suffered," he would say.*

 The oppressions seemed endless and the civil wars were merely an example of it.

Mustafa told me on countless occasions that he established the Amal organization to show how the Islamic Resistance Movement should be. However, he had many problems with the parties and groups that existed at the time. They said he was not Lebanese and that he was not one of them. Many people visited Imam Musa Sadr and spoke ill of Mustafa, though Mr. Sadr always retorted them. "I will not tolerate anyone who speaks ill of him," Imam Musa Sadr said. There was a kind of special spiritual connection between the two of them, and few people could understand it. "You know how much I like him? He is like a brother to me. He is my breath; he is me myself," Imam Musa Sadr said to me. He used strange words to describe Mustafa. Whenever he was talking, and Mustafa was entering the room, his attention shifted to him. He couldn't see anyone else anymore. His facial expressions were spectacular; sometimes he laughed, sometimes he cried, and how beautifully they hugged each other. They also had many disagreements, they debated with each other, but they respected each other despite their disagreements.

The first time I met Imam Musa after our marriage in Lebanon, he wanted to have a private conversation with me. "Ghada! Do you know who you have married? You have married a great man. You must be grateful for this blessing that God has bestowed upon you," he said. I was surprised by what he said. "I am grateful to him," I said. Then, I started to talk about Mustafa's moral qualities. He interrupted me and said, "Mustafa's temperament originates from his conscience; it comes from the reality of demeanor and conduct in the center of his heart. His socialization with us and others is in actuality a descent from his spiritual state to the realm of figures and ideas". He was sorry that those around us could not understand it. They thought his modesty was because of his inability, poverty, or loneliness. "I expect you to understand these issues," Imam Musa said.

I couldn't understand it then, but certain things happened as time went by which allowed me to recognize Mustafa more and more. I remember Israel had attacked the south of Lebanon, and the Jabal Amel School was in actuality Mustafa's military base. People had left the south. Even most of the young people in the Amal organization were angry. "We can't fight Israel. We are neither financially strong nor militarily equipped. Such a war is nothing but death for us. How could you keep us here?" they would say. "I won't make anyone stay here. Everyone is free to leave and save his own life. The only reason I'm staying is that I have relied on God and accepted his will. I will fight and defend this base as much as I can. In any case, I will not make anyone stay," Mustafa said. He spoke so calmly that I thought help was on the way, and he was probably being supported by someone. He talked to the children for some time more and then entered our room, which was in the institute. The institute was located on the heights overlooking the city of Tyre. I followed him and found him leaning against the window, looking outside. The sun was setting, sinking into the sea. The sky had turned crimson, and sunlight was reflecting off the sea waves. It was a beautiful scene. I saw him looking at the sight and crying. He cried a lot. I could even hear the stifled sound of his crying. I thought he was crying because he could feel how close to death we were after talking to the children with such spirit. "What's wrong, Mustafa?" I asked. It was as if he was mesmerized by such beauty. "Look how beautiful it is!" he said. Then he began to describe it.

The words he used were as beautiful as the scenery itself. I became outraged. "Mustafa, look at the other side of the city. What are you calling beautiful? Poor people have abandoned their cities; others have fearfully huddled in shelters, and you call all this beautiful? Why don't you look at the other side? What are you doing? People have lost everything, and so much blood has been shed, and you tell me, look how beautiful it is?!" I said. Even when the artillery shells exploded in the sky, he would say "Look how beautiful it is!" He laughed when I finished speaking. "In the midst of the glory, try to see the beauty. Many of these people have been martyred. They have lost their lives. You are looking at this from the perspective of glory. All of these things are God's mercy to turn their hearts back toward Himself. Some pains are filthy, but those that are tolerated for the sake of God are very beautiful," he said as he was leaning against the window with the utmost calmness. It was so strange to me that he was so carefree in the middle of the bombardment. He was aware of God's power and the beauty of sunset amidst death and destruction. He wasn't afraid of death at all. In one of his writings, he once wrote, "I attack the queen of death to embrace her, but she escapes from me. Dying and being sacrificed for the sake of God is the greatest pleasure one can achieve". He never went anywhere with bodyguards. "Well, now that you are not traveling with bodyguards, I'll be your bodyguard. I'll keep the Kalashnikov rifle loaded in case someone attacks you," I said. "No! God is my guardian. If that's my destiny, then neither I nor you and thousands of bodyguards will be able to change it," he said. He was like that in Lebanon. And when we went to Iran, he was the same in Ahvaz and Kurdistan, as well.

Chapter 3

A Stranger in Iran!

She recalled Imam Musa's words: "You have married a great man. God has bestowed upon you the greatest of His gifts." She always thought that the greatest blessing in one's life was to meet a great soul. But the philosophy of creation is based on the fact that the greatest blessings in life come with the greatest pains. Where is Mustafa now? Under the same sky, but far away, too far away from her... She closed her eyes and tried to think of Iran... Iran... Oh God, what if he doesn't come back? What should she do then? How could she leave Jabal Amel? How could she leave the Tyre Sea behind?

That day, when I bade farewell to Mustafa and returned to Tyre, I cried all the way driving to Tyre. For the first time, I realized that Mustafa was gone and that he might not come back. Can I go to Iran and leave Lebanon? That night was tough to bear. I was informed about the Islamic Revolution and what was happening in Iran from the very first day of our marriage, but this was like a long sleep. I didn't think it was possible. Many figures, including Dr. Beheshti[12], Sayyed Ahmad Khomeini[13], and other Iranian figures, came to Lebanon and took military training at the institute.

---

12. Ayatollah shaheed Sayyid Muhammad Hosseini Beheshti (1928-1981) was one of the greatest students of Imam Khomeini and a modern scholar in the religious context of Iran. After the victory of the Islamic Revolution, he was appointed as a member of the Council of Revolution. He was martyred in the explosion of the headquarters of the Islamic Republican Party, together with seventy-two members of the party.

13. Sayyed Ahmad Khomeini, known as Haj Ahmad Aqa (1946-1995), was Imam Khomeini's second son who administered the affairs of his father towards the end of his life. He passed away in 1995 at the age of forty-nine, five years after his father's demise.

I knew Mustafa was thinking about going back to Iran. Once, he had wanted to send me to Iraq to deliver a letter to Imam Khomeini and had even told me to learn Farsi very well. I knew that Imam Khomeini was in Paris, and when the revolution triumphed, we were all happy and celebrated it. But I had never given thought to the idea that Mustafa could return to Iran. I eventually caught on to the idea, but I never knew what the end result would be until one day Mustafa said, "We are going to Iran". He was with some Lebanese figures. "Are you going to come back?" I asked. "I don't know…," he replied. Mustafa traveled to Iran. The rest came back, but he didn't. He sent a letter explaining that Imam Khomeini had asked him to stay, so he had decided to do so and that his presence in Iran might be more beneficial than in Lebanon. Although I was happy that Mustafa went back to his home country and the revolution triumphed, but it was still very painful. Fifteen days later, I received Mustafa's second letter in which he had asked me to come to Iran. Deep in my heart, I wanted to stay in Lebanon, and I wasn't ready to live in Iran. We had nothing in Iran. I asked Mustafa about his responsibilities in Lebanon. We decided that he should stay in Iran, and I should stay in Lebanon and continue his work until the school was closed. "I don't want the children to think we have gone to Iran and abandoned them," Mustafa said. During that time, I would visit Iran almost once a month, and other than that we would talk over the phone. But I was constantly worried about what could have happened if life had gone on like this.

When the war in Kurdistan began, I was in Lebanon, and when I finally managed to get to Iran as soon as possible, I noticed that Mustafa wasn't waiting for me at the airport as usual. Instead, his brother came and told me that he was on a trip. That night, I heard the words such as Paveh[14] and Chamran on TV several times. I didn't understand Farsi, except for a few words. No one told me anything. I became really upset. I felt like something was happening, but the people around me said it was okay and that Mustafa would return. No one listened to me. I thought I was losing my mind, and my heart was in turmoil.

---

14. Paveh is an ancient Kurdish border town in Iran, in Kermanshah Province. It was a center of conflicts during the Kurdistan riots, which was liberated from the siege of riot forces, under the commandership of shaheed Mustafa Chamran.

The next day, I went to the office of the Prime Minister to meet Mr. Mehdi Bazargan[15]. There I found that something was wrong. Imam Khomeini's message had been announced, and people had taken part in a demonstration. Paveh was under siege. "I want to be with Mustafa. No one listens to me. They won't let me go," I told Mr. Bazargan.

> *The following day, Bazargan asked for Ghada and told her that Mustafa had sent for her and said that she should come. Ghada was so excited. She knew, from the very beginning, that Mustafa would never stop her from visiting if he knew she was there, even at war. Mustafa was ok with her traveling to Paveh, and he sent Mohsen Elahi to take her. She knew Mohsen from Lebanon, when he came to the institute and studied there.*

When I reached Paveh, the siege had ended, and the city had been liberated.

---

15. Mehdi Bazargan (1907-1995) was the first prime minister in the Islamic Republic of Iran and a serious opponent of the Pahlavi monarchy. Shaheed Chamran was a minister of defense in Bazargan's government.

Mustafa wasn't there, but I saw him the next day. He came wearing the same dusty war uniform. It reminded me of Lebanon. I thought Mustafa wouldn't have a Kalashnikov rifle and military uniforms in Iran. But I saw he was the same as before, as if it was another Lebanon. "I want to stay in Kurdistan to finish this. I sent for you because we have nowhere in Tehran, and it would be better if you stay with me here," he said. He asked me to be careful and write the story, especially for the newspapers in Arab countries. I wrote down every single word he said. I was with him in Kurdistan for about a month, from Paveh to Saqqez[16], from Saqqez to Miandoab[17], Nowsud[18],

---

16. Saqqez is a historical city in northwestern Iran in Kurdistan, dating back to ancient Persia. During the Iraqi Ba'ath regime invasion of Iran, the city was frequently attacked by the Iraqi army.

17. Miandoab is a city in northwestern Iran, located in West Azerbaijan Province. Nearly 850 warriors of the city were martyred during the Iraqi war on Iran, in defense of their Islamic homeland.

18. Nowsud is a Kurdish town in Iran in Kermanshah Province, which was occupied by the Iraqi regime for seven years.

Marivan[19], and Sardasht[20]. Most of the time, Mustafa was involved in military operations and I was alone. I didn't know how to speak Farsi. I would walk around, waiting for him to come. Sometimes, I would talk to the pilots since they could speak English.

Nowsud reminded me of Lebanon, of my memories. Nowsud's nature was so beautiful, and especially its mountains reminded me of Lebanon. Mustafa and I would go for a walk in such a beautiful nature, and he would talk about what was going on, about the Kurds seeking autonomy. "Why don't you grant them autonomy?" I asked. He became irate. "Our age is not the age of nationalism. Even if the Fars want to claim a country, I oppose them. In Islam, Arabs, Ajams (non-Arabs), Baluchis, and Kurds are no different. What matters is that the country (Iran) should have an Islamic flag," he said.

---

19. Marivan is a Kurdish city in west of Iran, located in Kurdistan Province on the Iraqi border. The city was victim to chemical bombardments by the Ba'ath regime in Iraq.

20. Sardasht is a Kurdish city in northwestern Iran, which fell victim to chemical attacks by the Iraqi Ba'ath army, in 1987 during the Iraqi war on Iran. After Hiroshima, it counts as the second largest victim of chemical weapons.

Most of our days in Kurdistan were spent in Marivan. There were no amenities and I didn't even have anywhere to sleep. Army, garrisons, and a few half-built houses, which were more like chambers than real houses, were all that were there. I would sleep on the ground in these chambers. I stayed hungry a lot of the time and even when there was food, watermelon and cheese were all that I could find to eat. It was very hard for me. One afternoon when I was alone, I sat on the ground and cried.

Ghada always tried her best to hide her tears from Mustafa. But on that day, Mustafa suddenly appeared and saw her crying. He came towards Ghada, knelt, and began to apologize. "I know your life shouldn't be like this. You had no idea you would end up like this. You can go back to Tehran if you want. But I can't. This is my path, and the revolution itself is in danger. Imam has commanded us to clear Kurdistan, and I will resist with all my heart until the end," he said. "Let's go back. I can't stay here," Ghada begged. "You are free; you can go back to Tehran," he said. Her eyes were filled with tears. "You know

that I can't go back without you. I don't know anyone here. I can't speak with anyone. Most of the time I look forward to seeing your return, and then I don't hear of you for two days," she said. Mustafa's palms were still on his knees as if he was performing tashahhud²¹. "If you decide to stay, do it for God's sake, not for me," he said.

I decided to stay until the end. However, when we returned to Sardasht, I joined the hospital team because I couldn't remain idle. There was so much trouble in Kurdistan. Mr. Taleqani²² passed away during those days and we returned to Tehran. I had a hard time in Tehran, and it was the first time I saw Mustafa in such a state of worry. *Munafeqin*²³ attacked him a lot. They had

---

21. Tashahhud is an obligatory part of prayers (salāt), which is performed by the worshiper.
22. Mahmoud Taleqani (4 March 1911 – 9 September 1979) An Iranian theologian, Muslim reformer, democracy advocate and a senior Shi'a cleric of Iran.
23. People's Mujahedin Organization (MEK), known in Iran as *Munafiqin* (Hypocrites), is a scandalous terrorist group that fled Iran in 1981, because of its conflicts with the religious beliefs of the Iranian people and the government, resulting in widespread

drawn a picture of him in newspapers with a firing tank on his glasses. It was such a horrible picture. I witnessed how sincerely he worked, how tirelessly he worked, and how much he starved. Yet, the newspapers created this kind of uproar. In my opinion, no one understood what Mustafa did. From that day on, I hated politics. "You must leave Iran. Let's go back to Lebanon," I said to Mustafa. But he stayed. "Don't think life will be easy just because I came and took up a post. As long as right and wrong exists and one doesn't remain quiet, there will be war," he said to me.

Finally, Paveh was liberated, and I returned to Lebanon. The mere occasional traveling back and forth between Lebanon and Iran was good for me, and Mustafa would tell me exactly what to do when I went back. He would ask me to take care of the school children and comfort each of the martyrs' families. He wrote them letters. "Tell them that I remember them and love them," he said. "Our friends! I don't want

---

assassinations and slaughters of the Iranian people and the officials of the Islamic Republic of Iran. Outside of Iran, it continues its terrorist and espionage activities against Iran.

them to think I have come to Iran, become a minister, and forgotten them," he said repeatedly.

Once in Lebanon, I heard that Ba'athist Iraq had invaded Iran and I became distraught. I was delighted after the war in Kurdistan ended. I thought the tears I shed there in loneliness had a positive outcome. In Kurdistan, I would pray with all my heart for the end of the war. I couldn't stand it anymore. My heart was hurting for Mustafa. I couldn't leave him, but I had the right to live in peace. I thought God would answer my prayers, and the war in Lebanon and Iran would finally end. Hearing about Iraq's invasion of Iran was traumatic for me. I knew Mustafa would be among the first people who would get himself there. The airport was closed, and I was trying to get to Iran as soon as possible. Finally, I entered Iran by military aircraft. In Tehran, I was told that Mustafa was in Ahvaz. Along with some others, we departed for Ahvaz by a C-130 plane.

> *Ghada's heart was in turmoil: Where is Mustafa? Is he okay? Will she see his lovely face again? The plane's engine caught fire, and all the fear and commotion around her made her more*

> *distressed. She opened Mustafa's last letter and started reading it:*
>
> *"I'm in Iran, but my heart is with you in the south, in the institute, in Tyre. I feel, I shout, I burn, and run with you under the bombardment and fire. With you, I feel I am moving towards death, towards martyrdom, towards meeting God with dignity. I feel I am always with you, even at the moment of martyrdom, even the last day before God. When you feel devoured by misery, hold my hands and feel that you are melting into my soul. Accept love with open arms. Hold the hand of love. Love turns misery into pleasure, death into survival, and fear into courage."*

Mustafa wasn't there when I arrived. I didn't know if he was still alive. The most difficult days were the first days of the war. There were very few people, maybe 15 or 17. In Ahvaz, we first went to Jundi Shapour University, known as Shahid Chamran University. Then, after the bombardments worsened, we were transferred to the governor's office. They were pure gentlemen, most of whom were martyred. When we were transferred to the governor's office, Mustafa was in Ahvaz

Roling and Pipe Mills Company, fighting against the enemies. I remember I lost him for two days. Those days were hard because I had no news of him. We were dispersed. The missiles fired were horrible. Wherever I went, I was told that Mustafa was looking for me. We couldn't find each other. Later on, he found out that we had been transferred to the governor's office, turned into irregular warfare headquarter. It was in Ahvaz that I became more acquainted with death.

> *The first time Ghada saw a morgue, she was in Kurdistan working in Sardasht hospital. In Lebanon, they had no such thing as a morgue. That day, when she was told that she had to take some martyrs' bodies from the morgue, she had no idea about the scene she would encounter. She was shown a room with walls full of drawers and was told that the martyrs were there. The person with her began to pull out the drawers…corpse, corpse, and corpse. Ghada was frightened. She fainted and fell to the ground.*

I got used to it a little at a time. In Ahvaz, I pulled out drawers and received the martyrs one by one. When I would go there at night, I would ask them about which corpse I should find the next day.

I worked in an Arabic radio station and sent Arabic messages during the first days of the war. Because of the bombardments, death completely surrounded us. I faced death in Ahvaz and it felt like hundreds of years. Several days would often pass by without news of Mustafa. I wouldn't be able locate him, but then, he would send me a small note saying: 'I'm leaving you for God's sake.' He did this in Lebanon, too, but it was tolerable there. But once in Sardasht, I didn't understand Farsi, in the middle of the army, war, and death, there came a note that said: 'I'm leaving you for God's sake,' and once the messenger left, I just waited for someone to come and tell me that he was gone. I was ready for such news and I prepared myself for everything to come to an end.

The day he was wounded, Asgari – one of those with Mustafa when Susangerd[24] was under siege – said Akbar was martyred, and Dr. Chamran was wounded. I was losing my

---

24. Susangerd is a city in Khuzestan in southwestern Iran, which was occupied by the Iraqi army during the Iraqi war on Iran, but at the command of Imam Khomeini and under the commandership of shaheed Chamran and Ayatollah Khamenei, it was soon liberated.

mind. "Where?" I asked. "The hospital," he replied. I couldn't believe it. I thought it was all over. When I arrived at the hospital, I saw that Mr. Khamenei[25] was there, and they were taking Mustafa out of the operating room. He was laughing and I was elated. I thought we were going to be transferred to Tehran and have some time to rest. "Will we go?" I asked Mustafa that night. "No, I won't. My comrades will be demoralized if I go to Tehran. If I can't fight on the front line, I can at least stay here and share in their difficulties.". This made me angry, I couldn't believe what he was saying. "Those who get wounded here, go and get taken care of. If you would like to be like the others, be like them in this situation," I said. Mustafa strongly opposed. "I can still do something. I can't leave my comrades. I have nothing to do in Tehran," he said.

He didn't even want to turn on the air conditioner. Ahvaz was extremely hot, and Mustafa's foot was in a cast. His skin

---

25. Ayatollah Sayyid Ali Hosseini Khamenei, a Shia religious authority and the present supreme leader of the Islamic Republic of Iran since 1989 after Imam Khomeini's demise. Prior to his current role, during the Iraqi war on Iran, he was the country's president.

was corroded and bleeding due to the hot weather. "How can I turn on the air conditioner while my partners are fighting on the front line in hot weather?" he said. He ate the same food as the others, and in Ahvaz, we had nothing to eat. "We can't go on like this. Mustafa is very weak. He's been bleeding. He is suffering from pain. I should cook for him myself," I said to Naser Farajollahi, who was with us at that time and was martyred later. I asked him to bring me a pressure cooker and I went to the city and bought some chicken to make Mustafa some soup. "Dr. Chamran will not accept it," Naser said. "We won't let him know. We'll tell him it's been made by the headquarters," I said. I dealt with things with emotion. Mustafa needed to regain his strength. I felt pain for him.

We took the cooker to the Green Berets' room because we had no stove. It was the army officers' room which was equipped with a refrigerator, stove, etc. "Anyone in the room who hears the cooker whistling, turn off the stove after half an hour," I said to Naser. Naser put the cooker on the stove. That day, officers had come from the garrison and had a meeting there. I was praying upstairs. We suddenly heard an explosion from the headquarters. We first thought an artillery shell had hit the base. The officers were running out of the room, and everyone thought they had received shrapnel wounds. Then I found out that the cooker had not whistled and exploded in the middle of their meeting. It was both funny and sad at the same time. "What happened? Was it Mrs. Chamran's cooker that exploded?" everybody asked. I didn't know how to tell Mustafa about what had just happened. I went back upstairs laughing. "Mustafa, I want to tell you something. Will you get upset?" I said. "No," he replied. "Promise me you won't," I said. I wanted to tell him about what happened before anybody else did. Then I told him the story, and he laughed and laughed. "What did you do in front of the officers? Why did you insist on giving me soup? Look what God did," he said to me.

Chapter 4

I Will Be Martyred Tomorrow

Had Ghada known Mustafa would do such a thing, she would not retreat, would stay in Ahvaz and be so hard on herself, and she would have never prayed for him getting wounded and shot in the foot! "Ghada has prayed that I get shot and be unable to move," Mustafa said, laughing. She couldn't tell anyone how much she loved Mustafa, how difficult it was for her to endure it, and that Mustafa was hers.

At that time, it was as if I had been lost in Mustafa's love rather than in God's. I told Mustafa to leave Iran and I was waiting for an excuse to get him out of the country. I felt there would be great danger, and I had to warn him about it, especially once the war in Kurdistan began. There was a disturbance in my heart. Waiting for something to happen is much more painful than the event itself. "Mustafa, you are mine," I said. He understood why I said that. "Every part of love is beautiful. You pay attention to ownership. I belong to God, so do you. This existence belongs to God," he said. "I wish you would get old right this moment. I am looking forward to seeing you as an old man, so neither a Kalashnikov rifle nor war could take you away from me," I wrote to him. "This is selfish, but I love your selfishness, it's an innate quality. But how come you don't endure the problems of life. I want you to be strong like a mountain, fluid and vast like a sea of eternity… Do you say property? Ownership? You are more valuable than property. I expect more from you. I see perfection, glory, and beauty in you. You should walk in God's path (the path of righteousness). You are a manifestation of God. You shouldn't be selfish. You are a soul. You should ascend to heaven and fly. How can I imagine you trapped in the prison of the night? You are the bird of the sanctum. You can cross all barriers. You can fly in the dark," he replied.

However, I didn't want him to be martyred until the night he asked me to be content with his martyrdom. That night, Mustafa was supposed to stay in Tehran. He had told me he would come back after two days. It was evening time, and I was sitting in the headquarters, in the operation room. It was actually Mustafa's room, and no one came in when he wasn't there. But the door suddenly opened. I was scared, wondering who was behind the door. Mustafa entered. I was surprised. He wasn't supposed to come back. "It seems you are not happy about my arrival. I have come for you," he said while looking at me. "No, Mustafa! You have never come back for me. You have come back for something work-related," I said. "Tonight, I have come back for you. Ask Ahmad Saeidi. Tonight, I was insisting on returning to Ahvaz. There was no plane. You know, I've never used a private plane. Tonight, however, I was insisting on coming back, so I took a private plane to be here," he said kindly as usual. I was wrought-up. "Mustafa! While I was walking by the Karun River, I was so overwhelmed with grief that I wanted to shout. I was so depressed. I felt even shouting by the river could not help me relieve my pain," I said. Mustafa listened. "There was so much love in me that even your arrival couldn't console me," I said. "You need a love bigger than me, and it's the love of God. You need to reach a stage of development where nothing satisfies you except for God and His love. Now I can go confidently," he said. At that moment, I didn't understand what he meant. At night, I went upstairs and as I entered the room, I saw Mustafa lying on the bed. I thought he was asleep and so I went towards him and kissed him. Mustafa was sensitive about some specific things. One day, after I tried to put his slippers in front of him, he became upset. He ran towards me, knelt, and kissed my hand. "You brought my slippers?" he said. That night I wondered why he didn't even move when I kissed his foot. I felt he was awake, closing his eyes, not saying anything. "I will be martyred tomorrow," he said. I thought he was joking. "Do you decide when to be martyred?" I said. "No, I asked God to make me a martyr, and I know he will answer me. But I want you to be content. If you're not content, I won't be martyred," he said. It was strange to me. "Mustafa, I won't be content, and clearly, it is out of your control. Well, I will be content if God wants you martyred, and I'll be waiting for that day. But why tomorrow?" I said. "I will leave here tomorrow, and I want you to be fully content with it," he said persistently. Finally, he obtained my consent. I didn't know how I gave him my permission. He gave me a letter which was his will. "Do not open it until tomorrow," he said. Then, he gave me two orders. "First of all, stay in Iran," he said. "Why should I do that? I have no one here," I said. "No! Returning after *Hijra*[26] is not permissible. We have an Islamic state here, and you have Iranian citizenship. You can't return to a country whose state is not Islamic, even if that country is your home country," he said. "So, what do all these Iranians do abroad?" I asked. "They're wrong. You shouldn't return to those customs again…ever!" he said. The second recommendation was that I should get married after his martyrdom. "No, Mustafa. After the death of Prophet Muhammad (s), his wives…," I said. "Don't say that. It's hearsay. I'm not the Prophet Muhammad (s)," he said while covering my mouth with his hand. "I know. I want to say that there was no one like him, and I won't find anyone like you, either," I said.

---

26. Ta'arrub ba'd al-hijra (literally: degression or becoming a Bedouin after immigration) is a religious term, referring to immigration to a land as a result of which one becomes shored of one's religious faith.

Ghada always loved to follow Mustafa in prayer, but Mustafa liked to say his prayers alone. "Your prayer will be annulled," he said to Ghada. She couldn't understand if he was joking or if he was serious. Yet, she followed him in some of her obligatory prayers. She noticed that after each prayer, he prostrated, rubbed his face on the dirt, and cried. Such lengthy prostrations! In the middle of the night, when he woke up for the night prayer, Ghada couldn't tolerate it. "Stop it. Get some rest; you look tired," she said. "If a merchant spends his savings, he will eventually go bankrupt. He should make a profit to live his life. If we do not say night prayers, we will go bankrupt," he replied. But she, who woke up most nights upon hearing his cries, never gave up. "What if those who are so scared of you find out that you cry so terribly… What sin have you committed? God has given you everything, even waking up at night is a blessing," she said. Then his cries turned into sobbing. "Shall I not thank God for this blessing?" he said. Why was she thinking about him using the past tense? Mustafa was with her. "You mean after you leave here

tomorrow, I won't see you anymore?" she said. "No!" he responded. She looked carefully at his face and then closed her eyes. "I must get used to seeing your face with closed eyes," she said.

The last night with Mustafa was unusual. I don't know how to describe it. The following day, when he wanted to go, I prepared his uniform and weapon and gave him some cold water to drink on the way. He took them from me. "You are such a nice girl," he said. Then several people suddenly entered the room, and I had to go upstairs. It was early in the morning, and the sky was not bright yet. As I turned on the light, the light went on and then suddenly out. It seemed that the light bulb burned out. "Mustafa will be gone forever today. This candle will cease to be lit," I thought to myself.

I just realized why he was so insistent that he would be martyred that noon. He was always serious. I felt confident that he wouldn't come back if he went. I ran to take my small pistol (colt) and went downstairs. I intended to shoot him in the leg to stop him from going. He wasn't in the room. I came to the headquarters' entrance, and he got in the car at the same moment. "I want to go after Mustafa," I cried, but they didn't let me go. They thought I had gone crazy; I had a pistol in my hand! Meanwhile, Mustafa had gone, and I didn't know what to do. I walked into the headquarters, went up and down the stairs, and thought about why he said those things to me. Can I bear the fact that he will be martyred and will never come back?

I cried a lot, bitterly. I was the only woman in the headquarters. There was a woman in Ahvaz named 'Khorasani', who was my friend. We worked together. Suddenly, God gave me peace of mind. "Well, Mustafa's body is supposed to arrive at noon. I should be prepared to face this scene," I thought to myself. I had a seal brown gown and a pair of pants. I put them on and went to Mrs. Khorasani. I was distraught. I told her about what happened the night before and that Mustafa would be martyred today and she got angry.

"Why are you saying this? Mustafa fights on the front lines every day. Why are you saying this? Why are you repeatedly saying Mustafa was? Mustafa IS!" she said. "But today, he will be gone forever," I said. I was still at her house when the phone rang. "Go pick up the phone because they want to inform us that Mustafa is gone," I said. "Now you'll see it is not true; it's just your imagination," she said. She picked up the phone. I was close to her, listening with all my heart to what she said. She just said, "No! No!"

Then, the guys came to take us to the hospital. "Dr. Chamran has been wounded," they said. I knew the hospital; I worked there. When I entered the yard, I turned back toward the morgue. I knew Mustafa had been martyred, not wounded, and he was in the morgue. I was aware that he had gone. I went to the morgue, and I remember when I saw his body, I said: "Allah, accept this sacrifice from us." At that moment, it was all over for me, worrying over Mustafa's martyrdom, getting wounded, etc. I hugged him and pleaded to God, on behalf of Mustafa's blood and body which was one of many in the morgue to not withhold His mercy from this nation now that Mustafa was gone. I felt that God eliminated many dangers because of a righteous man, who once walked on this land with such pure intentions.

When I saw Mustafa laid out in the morgue, I felt like he was finally resting in peace. Mustafa had a difficult life. He suffered from pain. He was harassed a lot.

Those last days, there were issues related to Bani Sadr[27], and Mustafa was under so much pressure. He cried, walked, and stayed awake at night. I felt he no longer could endure staying away from God. He had so much love in himself that, like a gentle soul, he wanted to fly away. The martyrdom of some of the best young people was difficult for him to bear. In that moment, as I saw Mustafa lying there with such comfort, I felt at peace as well. Then others came and didn't let me stay with him any longer.

I don't know why in Iran dead bodies are taken to morgues. In Lebanon, when someone passes away, the body is taken to the home of the deceased. Everyone gathers around the body, recite the Quran, and scent the body. It seemed strange to me why a dear one who has passed away should be discarded or kept in the morgue. "He is our dear one. He is our Mustafa. Where is he? What has changed? Why should he be kept in the morgue?" I shouted. But

---

27. Sayyid Abolhassan Bani Sadr was the first Iranian president after the 1979 revolution. Upon the Ba'ath Iraqi invasion of Iran, he failed to properly organize Iranian military forces and was thus subject to severe criticism by the people and revolutionary forces.

no one listened to me. The first night in Ahvaz was so painful for me. Everyone had gathered around me to sympathize with me, but I didn't need anyone. I felt so terrible, I just cried and cried. The following day, we returned to Tehran. Returning to Tehran was more difficult, because the last time Mustafa and I had come to Ahvaz from Tehran with the same C-130 aircraft. I remember the pilots asked him to sit with them. But he never left me alone, he stayed close to me. It was so painful remembering that I came with him and I had to go back with his dead body. I insisted that they open the coffin, but they didn't. The rituals and ceremonies broke me more than anything else. They deprived me even at those last moments. We went to the home of Mustafa's mother after we arrived in Tehran. After that, I didn't know where they took the body. I was at his mother's home, and people had gathered around me. "Where is Mustafa?" I asked. But no one answered me. "Since yesterday? Why? Aren't you Muslims?" I shouted. I was so restless. Then they told me that they were going to perform Ghusl on Mustafa's body in the morgue. "Mustafa is gone. Why are you doing this?" I said and cried. "We'll bring him back," they said. "If you don't, I'll go to the morgue and sit beside him to bid farewell until morning. Upon my insistence they brought Mustafa, and because we didn't have a home in Tehran, they took him to the local mosque in his childhood neighborhood to bathe him. He had lain peacefully. I put my head on his chest and talked to him in the mosque until morning. It was a beautiful night and a difficult farewell. The next day, they took Mustafa somewhere, and I didn't know where I got lost in the middle of the crowd. That night, I had to return alone. It was at that moment that I felt Mustafa was gone. In funerals, people are completely lost, they are unaware.

As soon as Ghada entered the prime minister's yard and saw the basement, a pain slashed through her heart and her knees became bent. "Mustafa, you left and now my back is broken," she murmured and leaned against the wall. She took a look at everything around her; how did these two years pass? She remembered the many times that she entered through this door for the pleasure of seeing Mustafa and his presence. She remembered how these young, humble soldiers stood at attention, as a sign of respect. Life… life had lost its meaning for her it was as if she had been detached

from her roots. She remembered Lebanon and that poetry of Hafez[28].

At that time, she didn't understand Farsi at all. She didn't realize what Imam Musa and Mustafa read together. Imam Musa himself explained what the fal-e Hafez[29] is to her, and then he took a fal-e Hafez for her. The fal said:

Ho! O wine bearer, pass around and offer the bowl (of love for God):

For love at first, appeared easy, but then befell the difficulties.

After Mustafa's martyrdom, I left the house (because the house belonged to the government), and I had nothing but the

---

28. Hafez; a Persian poet whose collected works are regarded as a pinnacle of Persian literature and are to be found in the homes of most Iranians, who learn his poems by heart and use them as proverbs and sayings to this day.

29. Fal-e Hafez (omens or divination or bibliomancy through Hafez's poems) is a practice among Iranians in which they randomly choose a poem from the collection of poems by Hafez Shirazi, the greatest Iranian poet, to foretell their future. The practice has no religious ground or rationale.

clothes I was wearing. I didn't even have any money to spend. It is typical for the deceased person's family to welcome and serve people in Iran, and I didn't know, it is not like this in Lebanon. I knew that people tried to have mercy on me by saying I was a foreigner, unfamiliar with their customs. I felt that the house was not mine and I had to go. But where? I stayed at my dear mother in law's house for a while, and some friends were with me. Each night, I slept in a different place, but mostly in Behesht-e Zahra[30] beside Mustafa's grave. I spent many tough nights. Lebanon was in chaos, our home had been bombed and my family had left the country. Fridays were the most challenging days of all. People like to stay with their families on Fridays, but I went to Behesht-e Zahra so that I didn't bother anyone. I felt heartbroken, in so much pain. "You didn't do right by me," I said to Mustafa.

By the time we had to leave Lebanon, we spent whatever we had on the school and in Iran we had nothing. Now Mustafa

---

30. Behesht-e Zahra is Tehran's largest cemetery, where many martyrs of the Islamic Revolution, martyrs of the Iraqi war on Iran, and many other Iranian political and religious figures are buried.

was gone, and I was stuck wondering where I should go. My life was like that for six months until Imam Khomeini (r.a) was informed about my situation. "Mustafa didn't work for the government. Whatever he did was because of my direct order. I'm responsible for looking after you," Imam said to me when we visited him. Then, 'the Foundation of Martyrs and Veteran Affairs'[31] accommodated me. There was nothing in the house. Jahed, one of Dr. Chamran's friends, brought me a mattress, a few plates, etc., until I was finally able to call my dad, and they sent me money.

It was because of such hardships that I felt Mustafa oppressed me. What I felt was purely sensory, though. After I thought about it, I realized Mustafa had no earthly possessions, but what he gave me was worth the whole world. Mustafa is everywhere, in peoples' hearts. I remember once I was at the airport coming back from Iran, when a high

---

31. Foundation of Martyrs and Veterans Affairs is a governmental institution that was established after the victory of the Islamic Revolution in Iran at the command of Imam Khomeini to support veterans, those injured in the war, and families of martyrs in Iran.

ranking Christian Lebanese officer saw my name (Ghada Chamran) on my passport and asked me if I was related to him. I said I was Chamran's wife. He was intrigued. "He was our enemy, he fought against us, but he was a decent man," he said. Then he followed me out of the airport. "Is there no car to pick you up?" He asked. "It doesn't matter," I said. He laughed and then said "That's right. You are Chamran's wife!"

Sometimes, she thought the reason why God tested her more than others was because she lived with Mustafa, with a miniature version of Imam Ali (a). "You are not Imam Ali (a), no one can be like him. The way he lived was unique to him, and no one else can be like him," she always said to Mustafa. "No. I suppose you might be wrong. Such thoughts will prevent Islam from evolving. The path is open. Prophet Muhammad (s) says his ummah (nation) can do whatever he does, everyone within their power," said Dr. Chamran with tears in his eyes.

Mustafa tried to have less than others wherever he went, whether in Lebanon, Kurdistan, or Ahvaz. In Ahvaz, we had nothing but our personal belongings. It's not customary for Lebanese people to take off their shoes and sit on the ground. When foreigners or relatives came to our house, I was too shy to tell them to take off their shoes. "I'm not saying that the house should be luxurious, but it should have at least some sofas so that we are not misrepresenting Islam, making people think Muslims are miserable and have nothing," I said to Mustafa. But he vehemently opposed it. "Why are we so obsessed with what others want or like? Why do we want to show we are nice by doing such things? These are our customs. Look how clean this floor is, neat and beautiful! This way, you will be less bothered by the dust particles of shoes that scatter on the carpet," he said. He was always reluctant to come to our luxurious house in Lebanon. We had some beautiful ivory statues that dad had brought from Africa. They made Mustafa upset, and together we broke them all. "What are they for? The Quran must be used for home decoration as an Islamic tradition, as simple as this," he said. After my mother told us that we didn't have money and that she would bring us home appliances, Mustafa became upset and said it was not a matter of money. It was a matter of his life that he didn't want to change. But like any other woman, I liked having an ordinary life. In Iran, we didn't have anything, either. All the things we had belonged to the government. "We should have something of our own. You say "oppressed", even the oppressed have spoons, forks, and plates of their own, but we don't. We will have nothing if you don't have a post," I said. Upon my insistence, he agreed to take the basement of the premiership, which belonged to servants. He used to sleep in his office before I came to Iran. We didn't even have the ordinary life that every husband and wife had. He even gave his salary to the children. "I would like to die while I have no earthly possessions but a few meters of a grave, and it would be much better if I don't have that, either," he said. Mustafa wasn't of this world.

> *He wasn't in this world, but he was present and influential more than when he was alive. And Ghada dreamt about him a lot. Last night, she dreamt about Mustafa sitting in a wheelchair, unable to walk. She ran toward him. "Mustafa, what happened to you?" She asked. "Why did you let this happen to me? Why did you keep silent?" he asked. "What happened?" she asked. "They have made a statue of me. Don't let*

them do this. Go break it!" he ordered. When she woke up, she didn't know what Mustafa meant. She inquired and heard that a statue of Mustafa had been made in the Shahid Chamran University of Ahvaz. She knew that one of the affluent, beautiful streets of Tehran has also been named after Mustafa. This was the apparent of the city, which of course, made her happy. But she wished the conscience of the town was the same too. She would see certain types of people on these streets and her heart would break. She was afraid of the day Mustafa turned into a mere name, and ... forgotten forever.

That's why I dreamt about the statue of Chamran. Sometimes I ask myself if it makes me happy if Iran is entirely named after Chamran. Do all these things make up for Mustafa's smile, his kindness? Never! However, the answer would be "yes" if Shahid Chamran University trains people like Chamran.

Mustafa is not the kind of person whose statue should just be made and displayed somewhere. This statue is a dead object, but Mustafa is alive in people's consciences and hearts. People are involved in the battle between good and evil, and they should be helped as God helped me. In Tehran, when I was lonely, I looked back into my past life. What did I have to do with Iran? I, the daughter of Jabal Amel! I always said that I would die if I were taken out of Jabal Amel, like a fish out of water. I couldn't imagine life out of the south of Lebanon and Tyre. "If I knew the revolution would triumph and we were supposed to return to Iran and leave Jabal Amel, I don't know if I would have agreed to the marriage or not," I said to Mustafa. But I came, and Mustafa even took my ID under the name of "Ghada Chamran" to stay in *Dar al-Islam*[32] (abode of Islam) and not return. I feel, especially when I am in Mashhad, that God, through that man, took my hand, showed me the way, and rescued me out of a fire that was burning me whole.

It could have been that I be far from Jabal Amel, in America, like my brothers and sisters. Occasionally, as I left Iran for Lebanon to visit my family and relatives, they would laugh at me. "Iranians are all

---

32. Dar al-Islam is every land in which the Islamic laws are being implemented.

enthusiastic about getting a green card. You are a U.S. citizen; why are you losing this chance?" they would say. "The greatest green card I have and that no one else has, is this green cloth from the holy shrine of Imam Reza (a) I have worn around my neck," I said to them. I feel this blessing with all my heart. A blessing for which even if I spent my whole life in prostration, I couldn't thank God enough for. With Mustafa, I moved from the material world into the spiritual world, from imagery into reality. I pray to God that I never stop making progress after Mustafa, as he himself prayed for me:

> *"Dear God! I ask you sincerely… Please be Ghada's protector, and don't leave her alone! I want to see her successful after my death. Dear God! I want her never to stop making progress after me. I want her to think about me, like a beautiful flower she found on the course of life and perfection, and she must ascend higher and higher on that path. I want her to think about me like a dimly burning, small candle that burned in the dark until it died out, whose light she enjoyed for a short period. I want her to think about*

> *me like a breeze that came from the spiritual sky, whispered in her ear the word of love, and then went toward the word of eternity."*

www.ingramcontent.com/pod-product-compliance
Lightning Source LLC
Chambersburg PA
CBHW030043100526
44590CB00011B/315